How Did That Get Here?

The Biography of Spices

Ellen Rodger

 Crabtree Publishing Company
www.crabtreebooks.com

Crabtree Publishing Company
www.crabtreebooks.com

For the Cannella women: Rose, Louise, and Marie, the original spice girls. —R.G.

Series editor: Carrie Gleason
Editors: Rachel Eagen, L. Michelle Nielsen
Design and production coordinator: Rosie Gowsell
Cover design and production assistance: Samara Parent
Art direction: Rob MacGregor
Scanning technician: Arlene Arch-Wilson
Photo research: Allison Napier

Photo Credits: Erich Lessing/Art Resource, NY: p. 5 (bottom);
Biblioteca Estense, Modena, Italy/Bridgeman Art Library: p. 15 (top);
Bibliotheque Nationale, Paris, France, Archives Charmet/Bridgeman Art
Library: p. 21; Bibliotheque Nationale, Paris, France/Bridgeman Art
Library: p. 4; Library of Congress, Washington D.C., USA/Bridgeman
Art Library: p. 25 (bottom); Osterreichische Nationalbibliothek, Vienna,
Austria, Alinari/Bridgeman Art Library: p. 19 (bottom); Private
Collection, Dinodia/Bridgeman Art Library: p. 13 (bottom left); Private
Collection, Roger Perrin/Bridgeman Art Library: p. 17 (top); David Butz:
p. 30; Theo Allofs/zefa/Corbis: p. 13 (top left); Archivo Iconografico,
S.A./Corbis: p. 16; Bettmann/Corbis: p. 22; Bojan Brecelj/Corbis: p. 1;
Vo Trung Dung/Corbis Sygma: p. 7; Lindsay Hebberd/Corbis: p. 8, p. 9
(top), p. 15 (bottom); Dave G. Houser/Corbis: p. 31; Zen
Icknow/Corbis: p. 29 (top); Earl and Nazima Kowall/Corbis: p. 5 (top);
Richard T. Nowitz/Corbis: p. 13 (middle right); Royalty-Free/Corbis: p. 9
(bottom); Brenda Tharp/Corbis: p. 12 (top right); Arthur

Thévenart/Corbis: p. 28; Nik Wheeler/Corbis: p. 26 (top), p. 27, p. 29
(bottom), cover; Alison Wright/Corbis: p. 26 (bottom); Rodolpho
Arpia/istock International: p. 12 (middle right); Sergey Kashin/istock
International: p. 11 (middle right); Greg Nicholas/istock International:
p. 11 (top left); Bart Sadowski/istock International: p. 10 (bottom right
top); John Sigler/istock International: p. 10 (bottom right), p. 12 (middle
left); Suzannah Skelton/istock International: p. 11 (bottom left), p. 12
(bottom right); Stephen Turner/istock International: p. 3; Iva Villi/istock
International: p. 11 (top right): Glen Vlasenko/istock International:
p. 10 (top right); The British Library/Topham-HIP/The Image Works:
p. 18; Mary Evans Picture Library/The Image Works: p. 14, p. 25 (top);
Topham/The Image Works: p. 19 (top); North Wind Picture Archives:
p. 17 (bottom), p. 20, p. 23, p. 24; Other images from stock cd.

Cartography: Jim Chernishenko: p. 6

Cover: A spice merchant in Egypt sells a variety of spices in his shop.

Title page: A woman from Zanzibar harvests cloves. Zanzibar, off the
coast of Africa, is the world's leading clove producer.

Contents: Pepper was one of the most valued spices in ancient times.
Through trade, pepper has become one of the most commonly used
spices today.

Crabtree Publishing Company

www.crabtreebooks.com   1-800-387-7650

Cataloging-in-Publication Data
Rodger, Ellen.
    The biography of spices / written by Ellen Rodger.
        p. cm. -- (How did that get here?)
    Includes index.
    ISBN-13: 978-0-7787-2484-1 (rlb)
    ISBN-10: 0-7787-2484-0 (rlb)
    ISBN-13: 978-0-7787-2520-6 (pbk)
    ISBN-10: 0-7787-2520-0 (pbk)
    1. Spice trade--History--Juvenile literature. 2. Spices--Juvenile
    literature. I. Title. II. Series.
    HD9210.A2R63 2005
    382'.41383--dc22   2005019023
                                                LC

**Published in
the United States**
PMB 16A
350 Fifth Ave.
Suite 3308
New York, NY
10118

**Published
in Canada**
616 Welland Ave.
St. Catharines
Ontario, Canada
L2M 5V6

**Published in the
United Kingdom**
73 Lime Walk
Headington
Oxford
OX3 7AD
United Kingdom

**Published
in Australia**
386 Mt. Alexander Rd.
Ascot Vale (Melbourne)
VIC 3032

Contents

4   What are Spices?

6   From Whence They Came

10 Types of Spices

14 The Ancient Spice Trade

18 Medieval Spices

20 Merchant Companies

22 New World, New Spices

24 The American Spice Trade

26 A Nutmeg Farm

28 Harvesting Other Spices

30 Spice Trading Today

32 Glossary and Index

What are Spices?

Almost everything people eat today is flavored by spices. Spices are the seeds, fruit, roots, or bark of plants that once grew only in a few places on earth. For thousands of years, spices such as pepper, cloves, nutmeg, and cinnamon have been used to make medicines, perfumes, flavorings for food and drinks, and **balms** for wrapping the dead. Spices have changed the way people eat, how they live, and where they live. The greed for spices and the wealth they brought, launched ships of exploration in the 1400 and 1500s, and fueled brutal battles for control of territory all over the world.

Seeds and Twigs

Spices are parts of plants, but they are also important commodities, or items sold on established world markets. Spices are often ground, or mixed with other spices to create seasonings that flavor foods and preservatives that slow or prevent food from rotting. The market for spices is old. People have been trading spices for thousands of years.

▼ *Pepper was one of the most widely traded spices in ancient times. Today, black pepper is the top selling spice in North America.*

4

Demand for Spices

In ancient times, spices were important medicines. They were believed to help everything from upset stomachs, to toothaches, headaches, and infections. The sap, or resin, of trees is also considered a spice. Resins were used for making perfumes. Spices were even mixed into preparations, or potions that were thought to make people fall in love. Spices were so valuable that they were used to pay rents, and **dowries**. Today, people still value spices because they make foods taste better and their scents are pleasant. Billions of dollars worth of spices are grown and traded throughout the world every year.

(left) In some places around the world, spices are an important part of the economy. In Sikkim, India, cardamom is the state's most important crop.

Commodities

A commodity is something produced for sale that has value on a market. Some commodities are traded, or exchanged, at commodity markets, or exchanges, in the world's major cities. The New York Mercantile Exchange and the New York Commodities Exchange are private companies that trade commodities and determine price. If a product trades for a high price at a commodities exchange, it means people will pay a high price for it at markets and in stores.

At one time, spices were hard to get and many were very expensive to buy. Wealthy people had fancy spice boxes for keeping their spices.

From Whence They Came

Many of the world's most **coveted** spices originated, or first grew, in tropical areas of the world. The tropics are the areas just north and south of the equator. The spices grew wild and, over thousands of years, were cultivated, or grown as crops. Their distance from Europe and the fact that they could not be grown in areas of the world with harsh winters, made many spices **exotic** and desirable. Ancient trade routes carried spices from one part of the world to another. Over time, spices that originated in Asia were grown in Africa and the Caribbean. Spices that came from Central America were brought to Asia and Africa and planted there.

Where are they Grown Today?

Today, some countries specialize in growing specific spices. Guatemala, a country in Central America, is the world's biggest exporter of cardamom. Cardamom is a seed of a plant **native** to India and was not grown in Guatemala until the late 1900s. The tiny Caribbean island of Grenada is one of the world's top growers of nutmeg. Nutmeg is the seed of an evergreen tree native to Indonesia, half a world away from Grenada. It was brought to Grenada by the British in 1782, and was grown on **plantations** using slave labor. After slavery was officially abolished, or ended, in the **British Empire** in 1838, nutmeg continued to be a number one **export** for the island.

Spices have traveled a variety of routes to where they are grown today.

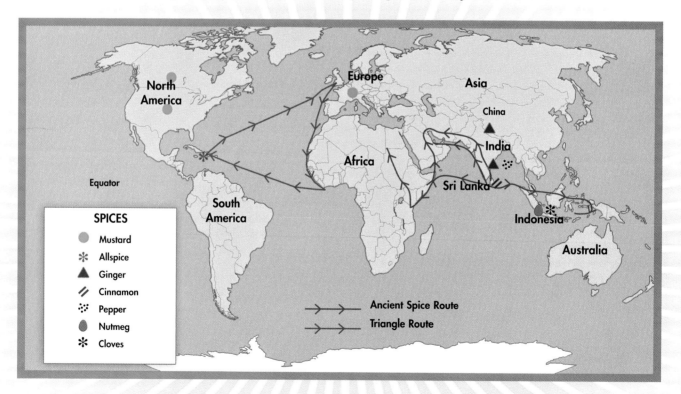

6

Spices of Europe

Some spices, such as anise, fennel, and saffron are native to Europe. Europeans have been using these spices as medicines and to flavor foods for thousands of years. Saffron is the dried yellow **stigmas** of a crocus flower. It is the most expensive spice in the world and comes from the Mediterranean. Anise is the dried, licorice-tasting fruit of an **herb**. Fennel is a seed that also tastes like licorice. These herbs are now grown throughout the world.

King of Spices

One of the world's best known spices, pepper, was loved by the ancient Romans. The Romans were a trading and **conquering** people who lived in what today is Italy. They traveled over land and sea to reach the source of the pepper plant in India. Pepper was so popular it was called the "king of spices." Today, pepper is grown in many areas of the world, including India, Indonesia, Malaysia, Brazil, and some African countries.

Spices in Africa

The ancient Greeks and Romans loved a spice called silphium. So much of it was used that the plant from which it came became **extinct** thousands of years ago. Silphium was a resin from the root of a plant that grew wild only in northern Africa. Many other spices came from the continent of Africa, including many types of cumin and a type of cardamom that was so prized in Europe it was called "grains of paradise." Early spice trade routes ran through Africa and over time, many of the spices brought from Asia by traders were planted in Africa. To this day, these spices still grow in parts of Africa.

Black pepper is the dried unripe berry, or peppercorn, of a vine called the **Piper nigrum.** *Pepper vines wrap around trees as they grow.*

The Spice Islands

The Spice Islands, or the Moluccas, is a collection of small islands in what today is Indonesia. The Spice Islands were given their name because early explorers knew that they were a paradise where spices grew wild or were farmed. The volcanic soil of the islands is very **fertile** for growing spices. Many different spices originated in the Spice Islands, including cloves, mace, and nutmeg. Cloves were brought to ancient Europe by the Arabs, a great trading people from **Arabia**. Today, cloves are grown in Indonesia as well as other tropical areas, such as the island of Madagascar off Africa's southeastern coast, Tanzania, Sri Lanka, Malaysia, and Grenada. Mace and nutmeg are still grown in the Moluccas, but today they are also grown in Sri Lanka and Grenada.

(background) Clove trees grow around a village in Java, Indonesia.

India and China

India and China are home to a number of spices. Ginger, the root of an herb, was thought to have originated in both countries. In the past, ginger was prized for its ability to calm an upset stomach. Licorice root is thought to have come from China, as did a spice called star anise and fagara, a spicy berry also called Chinese pepper. The spices cumin, fenugreek, and cardamom are thought to have come from India. Sri Lanka, a large island located south of India, was the original source of cinnamon. Cinnamon is still grown in Sri Lanka today but has also been **transplanted** to several other parts of the world. Cassia, a spice similar to cinnamon, is native to northern Myanmar, a country in Asia formerly known as Burma. Today, cassia is grown for **commercial** use in China, Vietnam, Indonesia, Myanmar, and Central America.

(above) Spices that once grew only in India and China are now grown around the world. Other spices, such as saffron, which originally grew in Europe, are now grown in South Asia.

New World Spices

In the 1400s, European explorers began looking for sea routes to the spice centers of the world in Asia. On their journeys they stumbled upon the continents of North and South America and learned about the plants and spices that grew there. Vanilla, chocolate, and chili peppers originally come from Mexico but are now grown in other areas of the world. Allspice, a spice that is the berry of an evergreen tree, is native to the Caribbean and is still grown there today. Many spices that were native to Asia were brought to the Caribbean, Central, and South America to be grown on plantations.

▲ Grenada's flag features a nutmeg fruit. In September 2004, Hurricane Ivan devastated the country's spice-growing industry. Over 90 percent, or 500,000, of the country's nutmeg trees were destroyed or damaged.

9

Types of Spices

Hundreds of years ago, traders sailing to Indonesia's Spice Islands smelled the fruit of the cloves and the nutmeg trees before they even reached them. The pungent spice aroma was so strong it carried across water. Today, as in the past, the most valued spices are often those grown only in specific geographical areas. Black pepper, cinnamon, nutmeg, and cloves are only grown in tropical climates with plenty of sunshine, rain, and fertile soil. Other spices can be grown in **temperate** climates.

Black Pepper ▲

Black pepper is a climbing vine or tree that is native to southern India. Pepper trees grow in hot, tropical climates that allow for year-round growth. In the wild, and when grown or cultivated, the pepper tree vine clings to taller trees and grows to about ten feet (three meters) tall. Pepper is the fruit, or berry, of the tree.

Cinnamon ▲

Cinnamon is the bark of the *cinnamonum verum* tree which is native to Sri Lanka, an island country located south of India. Cinnamon is grown today in Java, and in India. Other types of trees produce bark that is similar to cinnamon, including cassia. Much of what is sold as cinnamon in North America is actually not cinnamon at all, but the bark of the cassia tree. Cassia is red-brown in color, while cinnamon is paler brown.

Nutmeg and Mace ▲

Mace and nutmeg are the kernel and seed of the same evergreen tree.

Saffron ⌄

The crocus flower from which saffron is harvested is grown in Europe and Asia.

Cloves ⌃

Cloves are the small, nail-shaped flower buds of an evergreen tree.

Cardamom ▸

Cardamom is one of the most ancient and highly valued spices in the world. Cardamom pods are the fruit of a plant that grows wild in India and Sri Lanka. Today, it is also cultivated in Guatemala, Tanzania, and Vietnam. The small green pods are harvested and preserved green, bleached white, or dried brown. Commercially grown cardamom plants bear fruit for 10 to 15 years and the fruits ripen from September to December. On some plantations where cardamom is grown, special drying rooms are used to dry and store the pods. The tiny seeds inside the cardamom are what flavor foods. Today, cardamom is the third most expensive spice, after saffron and vanilla.

Coriander ◂

The seeds of coriander, an herb, is used as a spice. The herb can be grown in backyard gardens or on small-scale farms.

Mustard ▶

Mustard is used to flavor foods. In the Middle Ages it was also used to make medicines and balms, such as mustard plaster for colds and flu. Mustard is native to southern Europe and is now grown commercially on farms throughout Europe and North America. The small, pale or black seed of the mustard plant are harvested by machine when they are ripe but before they burst. Once harvested, the pods are dried and then **threshed.**

Ginger ▼

Ginger is the root of a tropical plant .

Star Anise ▶

Star Anise is the hard, star-shaped seedpod of the anise bush.

All in One: Allspice ▶

On Christopher Columbus' second voyage to North America, he came across a tree growing in the Caribbean that produced a berry he thought was pepper. He was so excited about this discovery that he even called the berries *pimienta*, the Spanish word for pepper. What Columbus found on the islands was not pepper, but allspice, the berry of an evergreen tree native to the Caribbean. The English name for the tree and its berry explains how it tastes like cloves, cinnamon, mace, and nutmeg all together. Today, allspice is grown commercially in Jamaica and on other Caribbean islands. The allspice tree grows to about 29 feet (nine meters) tall on farms and plantations. Allspice trees can bear fruit for up to 100 years.

Gums and Resins

Frankincense is a gum from a tree called *Boswellia sacra*, which grows only in southern Arabia. Myrrh is the resin of a tree called *Commiphora myrrha*, which grows in Yemen and Saudi Arabia, and in Somalia in northeastern Africa. To the ancient **Hebrews**, Egyptians, Romans, Greeks, Chinese, and Arabs, frankincense and myrrh were as valuable as gold. They were traded like spices and were burned in religious ceremonies and used as medicines. Myrrh was also used to spice wine.

(left) Most aromatic resins and gums are tapped from trees, such as eucalyptus trees, where workers slice into the bark and collect the sticky resin that drips from the cut.

Perfumes

Aromatics were used in ancient times, and are still used today for making perfumes and **incenses**. Aromatics from animal sources, such as musk, taken from the **glands** of male musk deer, and ambergris, a **secretion** from the **intestines** of sperm whales, were also popular in ancient times, especially in perfume making. Camphor was once one of the most sought after aromatics. It was used to preserve dead bodies. Camphor comes from the bark of a tropical tree. Today it is still used in drugs and preparations to help stop itching. Camphor's unique smell perfumes moth balls. Aloeswood is the resinous wood of an evergreen tree that grows in Asia. It is still used today in incense. Gum benzoin is a resin from a tree native to parts of Asia. It is used in medicinal ointments.

(above) Aromatic resins, such as frankincense, are burned for their pleasant scent.

(left) Sandalwood is a popular ingredient in perfumes and incenses. It is the root of a tree that is native to Indonesia.

The Ancient Spice Trade

Thousands of years ago, the ancient Chinese used ginger in medicines and to flavor foods. The ancient Chinese traded with seafaring people from Indonesia and Malaysia for spices they did not grow. The ancient Egyptians used spices and resins to embalm their pharaohs, or kings, and other **nobles** more than 4,000 years ago. Some spices they grew themselves, such as anise, mustard, and caraway. They traded with peoples to the south and in Arabia for the other spices they needed. The spices were hauled by camel caravan from southern Arabia, north to Mecca, in what is today Saudi Arabia, and then to Egypt.

Arab Traders

The Arabs were one of the first great spice traders. They brought spices from Asia and southern Africa to the Egyptians and other ancient peoples, including the Romans and the Greeks. The Arabs dominated the spice trade from about 960 B.C. to 1100 A.D. Spices were an excellent commodity to transport. Unlike fresh fruit or vegetables, spices did not spoil or rot, and unlike ceramics, they did not shatter. Arab traders traveled directly to the source of the spices in India, China, and later, the Spice Islands of Indonesia. The Arabs were among the first peoples to trade directly for long-distance goods.

▼ *The ancient Romans and Greeks used spices in foods, medicines, in tributes to their gods and leaders, and for burning in religious temples. They purchased huge amounts of spices from spice traders.*

▲ *To keep control of their spice trade, Arab traders kept their sources secret. They told fantastic stories about the origins of the spices to frighten people and prevent them from buying their spices directly from the source.*

By Sea and by Land

The Arabs followed several overland ancient spice-trading routes to transport spices from China or India through mountains and deserts to Central Asia and to Europe. The overland caravans were enormous, with up to 4,000 camels carrying goods, traders, water, and food. The Arabs also built great fleets of sailing ships to sail to the source of the spices. They crossed the Indian Ocean by following the monsoons, seasonal winds that brought their ships to India and Indonesia in summer. In the winter, the winds shifted direction and brought the Arabs back to their home ports, or to ports in East African trading cities.

(right) The ancient desert city of Petra, in Jordan, was a spice and resin trade city.

Trading Cities

Many stops along the spice routes became thriving, and wealthy trading towns and cities. The Indian cities of Kochi and Surat were centers for the trade in spices on the Indian coast of the Arabian Sea. Spice traders and other merchants settled there and built homes, and temples, or religious buildings. The great caravans stopped to feed and water their camels in places like Kashgar, an oasis city in what is today northern China. Other cities across Asia, such as Samarkand in present-day Uzbekistan, became places where merchants bargained for spices with the caravans. Arab traders sold the spices at markets in ancient Nineveh; Babylon in present-day Iraq; Carthage, in present day Tunisia; Egypt, and Rome.

Ancient Aromatics Trade

In addition to trading spices, ancient peoples also traded aromatics. Frankincense and myrrh were aromatic plant products that ancient peoples desired. Several other aromatics, gums, and resins were also popular enough thousands of years ago to spark a profitable trade. Ancient aromatics used as medicines and in making perfumes included aloeswood, sandalwood, gum guggal, gum benzoin, camphor, and balm of Gilead, or balsam of Mecca. Arab traders brought the fragrant spices and resins from all over Arabia, Asia, and Africa, by ship and camel caravan to the Middle East and Europe.

Roman and Greek Trade

Around 100 A.D., the ancient Romans discovered the source of pepper was in India and they began to sail there from Egypt to trade directly. The journey took two years and many Roman ships were lost in the quest for spices. The Romans did not know that the journey could be shortened by following the monsoon winds. When they began to use the monsoon route, the journey was shortened by a year.

▼ *The three wise men brought gifts of gold, frankincense, and myrrh to Jesus Christ to celebrate his birth.*

Bearing Gifts

The Bible, the **Christian** holy book, tells the story of three ancient kings visiting **Jesus Christ** as a child and bringing him gifts of frankincense and myrrh. The kings were said to be from the "orient," or ancient Arabia and the gifts showed their awe and respect for the child. The valuable resins were used as medicines and burned in religious ceremonies. Some ancient peoples used frankincense as an incense to cover the smell of burning flesh when they cremated, or burned their dead.

▲ *The story of Sinbad the Sailor from the ancient Arabian book,* **A Thousand and One Nights,** *is the story of a spice dealer who had many adventures at sea, including shipwrecks and being marooned on an island.*

Spreading Spice

Ancient Rome was an **empire**, and over time, the Romans expanded their territory across Europe from present-day Turkey in the east, as far as England in the west. They brought their passion for spices such as pepper, cumin, anise, and caraway with them across the empire. Eventually, the Europeans who they conquered also developed a taste for the foreign spices. Around 400 A.D., the Roman empire slowly crumbled, but the desire for spices remained. Rome began to lose its power and was attacked by invaders. In 408 and 409 A.D., one group of invaders, the Visgoths, threatened to sack the city of Rome if a ransom of gold, silver, silk, and 30,000 pounds of pepper was not paid. Pepper was so desired that its value was the same as gold. Rome paid the hefty ransom, but a year later, the city was sacked. The city of Constantinople, in present-day Turkey became the capital of the eastern empire and spice trade routes made their way to that city instead.

Trading Religion

The early spice trade brought the religion of Islam to Asia, India, Africa, Indonesia, and beyond. Islam is the religion followed by Muslims, who believe in one god, called Allah. Muslims believe Allah spoke to the prophet Muhammad, who founded a religion based on Allah's word. The prophet's first wife, Kadijha, was the widow of a wealthy spice merchant. Kadijha's wealth and prestige made it easier for Muhammad to spread the word of Allah throughout Arabia, using the well-known spice routes. After Muhammad's death, Muslim Arab traders continued to spread the religion throughout their trading routes.

Medieval Spices

In the early Middle Ages, Europeans had little to trade with the Arabs for the spices and the prices went up. Only very wealthy Europeans could afford spices. Spices that could be grown in Europe, including cumin, saffron, and mustard, were grown in fields and plots. The exotic spices that trickled in through trade were so highly valued that they were heavily taxed.

Crusades and the Spice Trade

Beginning in 1095, European Christians mounted a series of quests for territory in the holy lands, in present-day Israel and Palestine. The quests, called the Crusades, were aimed at taking control of the holy city of Jerusalem from the Muslims who also considered the city holy to their religion. Many of the crusaders settled in the holy land. Others returned home, bringing spices they had bought in the holy lands. They used the spices in cooking and for medicines. Soon, other Europeans also desired the spices.

Trading Centers

During the Middle Ages, the Italian **city-states** of Genoa and Venice became major ports for the spice trade. The merchants and rulers of the city-states made trade agreements with Arabs who brought spices from Asia. Merchants and traders in Venice and Genoa became very wealthy from the agreements. Venice and Genoa were almost constantly at war for control of the trade.

A New Leader

In 1308, Venice defeated Genoa and controlled the spice trade in Europe for another 100 years, shipping out European gold, silver, saffron, and wool, in exchange for pepper, ginger, cloves, cinnamon, and nutmeg. Venice's control of the European spice trade, called a monopoly, made other countries want to trade for spices.

▼ *Spices were used as medicine in the Middle Ages. The patients from this medieval illustration were burned with hot irons, which created boils on the skin. The boils were then rubbed with spices.*

Battles for Control

In the late 1400s, European countries launched voyages of discovery. Portuguese explorer Vasco da Gama returned after a sea voyage to India with his ship full of spices. Several other Portuguese explorers followed da Gama's path and Portugal established a direct trading relationship with India. In the early 1500s, the Portuguese began setting up work **colonies** in Sri Lanka, and in the Moluccas. They forced the people of the islands to grow spices that only the Portuguese could sell. Spice cargoes were sent to Lisbon, Portugal where Dutch traders had **concessions** that allowed them to take the spices and sell them in northern Europe. Other European countries also sent ships of exploration to find spices. Spain set up a spice-trading empire in Asia and Indonesia. The Spanish fought with the Portuguese over territory and eventually took over Portugal's spice trade. The Spanish king decided to cut the Dutch concessions and remove them from the trade entirely. In return, the Netherlands, then under the control of Spain, declared independence and in 1595, launched its own fleet to the Spice Islands.

▼ Explorer Vasco da Gama sailed down the coast of Africa, around the Cape of Good Hope, to India and back to Europe with spices.

What is a Monopoly?

A monopoly is a market where there are many buyers for a product or commodity, but only one seller. The seller can charge a hefty price because there is nowhere else the buyer can purchase the commodity. In the spice trade, the Arabs held the first monopoly, where they could charge high prices for spices in Europe because there was no other seller of spices to compete with. The Portuguese spice trade monopoly continued until the Spanish, and finally the Dutch took control.

Merchant Companies

The Dutch East India Company was formed in the early 1600s to control the Netherland's spice trade with Asia. In Amsterdam, a storehouse and docks were built to house the trade goods.

From the 1400s, many European countries grew wealthy by controlling the resources of territories they conquered or colonized. The money gained from the trade in spices, sugar, timber, and furs created vast empires for Britain, France, Spain, and the Netherlands.

Land Grab

The spice trade made those who participated in it ruthless. Royalty and merchants all wanted to make money on the trade. European kings and queens granted trading rights, or charters, to territory they believed was rightfully theirs in lands that were thousands of miles away.

Trading Rights

Sending ships from Europe to Asia and the Spice Islands was expensive. Groups of merchants banded together to finance, or pay for, expeditions. If the ships were not lost at sea, and made it back to their home ports, the merchants could count on making a lot of money. In 1602, the United East India Company, a Dutch company, was formed and given the right to wage war with Spain in the Moluccas and areas that became known as the East Indies. Through force and power, the company established a Dutch spice monopoly that lasted over 150 years.

Trade and Treaties

England ventured into the spice trade by granting charters to trading companies in the East Indies and North America. England and the Netherlands signed treaties, or agreements, to work together through their trading companies and divide the spice trade wealth, but the treaties were broken repeatedly. Trading companies fought battles for territory, took rival traders from other countries hostage, or took over their territories and sometimes killed their competition.

United East India Company

The United East India Company took hold of the spice trade by changing the way trading was done. They forced the kings and leaders of spice-growing islands to grow only one crop and buy the rest of what they needed from them. This made the islands dependent on the trading company for food and even their clothing. Islanders who openly resisted the United East India Company's total control were killed.

Keeping Control

The company forced Chinese and Arab traders out of the market. The native peoples of the islands became spice-producing slaves. The United East India Company even **manipulated** the spice market to keep prices high. When they produced too much cinnamon in their colonies, they burned the spice instead of selling it at a lower price. The Company's Dutch monopoly continued until around 1770, when a French botanist smuggled nutmeg and clove trees out of the Spice Islands. The spices were successfully grown in tropical French colonies. The British also planted clove and nutmeg trees in their Caribbean and Asian colonies in the late 1700s in order to take a share of the market.

▼ *Merchant companies used the labor of local peoples to harvest spices in the areas where they set up colonies.*

21

New World, New Spices

The European desire for spices and greed for money and territory launched many ships of exploration in the 1500s. On his three voyages to the New World, Christopher Columbus believed he would find a new western route to the spice markets of Asia.

Claiming New Territory

Columbus ventured into the Caribbean by chance when sailing west from Spain. Many explorers followed Columbus in charting a westward course from Europe to the Spice Islands. They did not find a sea route to Asia, but the lands they did find were claimed for the major European powers in the 1500s: Spain, France, Portugal, the Netherlands, and Britain.

Got it, Stamped it!

Over time, colonies were established in the New World. Portugal claimed Brazil, and Spain claimed territory in North America, including Mexico and areas to the north. England and France claimed land in what is today the United States and Canada. The islands of the Caribbean were claimed by many nations. Fruits, vegetables, spices, and animals found in the new territories of North, Central, and South America were brought back to Europe and also spread throughout European colonies in Asia and Africa. In turn, the fruits, vegetables, spices and animals of other areas of the world, were brought to the New World. Historians have called this process the Columbian Exchange.

The British East India Company was established through a royal trade charter in 1600. The company virtually ruled India, a top cotton, silk, tea, and spice producer, until 1858. The British continued to rule India until its independence in 1947. Many Indians worked for the British merchant company.

Slavery and Indentured Labor

Spices and other commodities such as sugar and cotton were brought from Old World colonies to New World colonies or territories. To grow spices on their plantations, European colonists used slaves. In the Moluccas, and other original spice-producing islands, the colonists enslaved the local inhabitants. Slaves lived brutal and short lives growing and harvesting spices. They were beaten, half-starved, and they suffered from sickness and disease. Slaves were also taken from Africa and forced to work on Caribbean spice plantations. When the trade in slaves ended on many of the island colonies in the early 1800s, **indentured laborers** were taken away from colonies in one part of the world and brought to work in colonies far away. Planters in the British West Indies for example, imported indentured laborers from India to work on plantations.

(background) Before Columbus, tomatoes, potatoes, chili peppers, and allspice were unknown in Europe and Asia.

The American Spice Trade

The city of Salem, Massachusetts, on the East Coast of the United States, was once a major spice-trading port. In the mid-1700s, Salem was a bustling port. Ships from Salem began sailing to Asia in 1785, after a ship bound for China returned with enough spices, including cassia, to make its owner, Elias Hasket Derby, very rich. Derby became so rich that he was said to be America's first millionaire.

Voyages to the Spices

In 1796, Jonathan Carnes was the first in a long line of Salem sea captains to chart a direct course to Sumatra, in Indonesia. Carnes and other ship's captains made many voyages to the East Indies to trade for spice. The goods were housed in wharves and transported all over America, and to Europe, where spices were in demand.

Businessmen in Salem count their money while planning future spice-trading voyages.

Center of Trade

Salem remained the center of the American spice trade for over 100 years. Hundreds of ships sailed from Salem to the East Indies, India, and China. Pepper was the most popular spice because it was resold for high prices. The pepper trade made great wealth for the government as well as spice merchants, wharf owners, and sea captains. The government charged import duties, or a tax, on commodities and goods. Salem exported 7.5 million pounds (3.4 million kilograms) of pepper a year by the early 1800s. American domination of the spice market came to an end in the late 1800s, as pirates began to attack American spice ships. The United States government decided it could not protect the ships in foreign waters, so the trade dwindled. Salem lost its biggest trade and the port's importance dwindled as it was replaced by bigger ports in Boston and New York.

▲ *Elihu Yale was a wealthy governor of Madras, India, who made his fortune in the spice trade. Yale was born in Boston and after he became wealthy, was asked to support a new university in 1701. Yale gave the school money, and eventually it was named after him.*

▼ Slaves were treated as human property. They were branded, or scarred, with a hot iron to show who they belonged to.

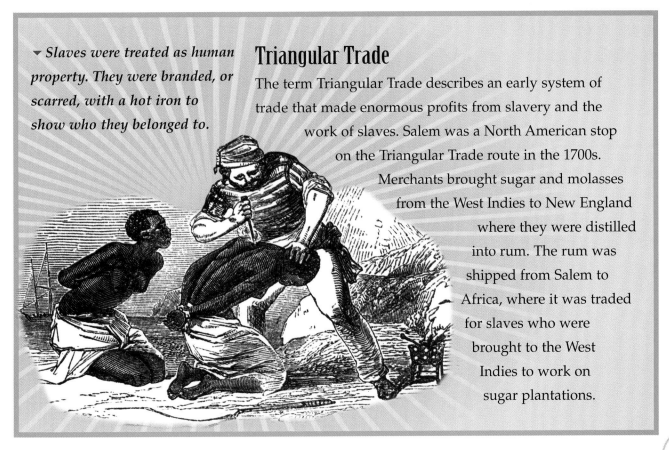

Triangular Trade

The term Triangular Trade describes an early system of trade that made enormous profits from slavery and the work of slaves. Salem was a North American stop on the Triangular Trade route in the 1700s. Merchants brought sugar and molasses from the West Indies to New England where they were distilled into rum. The rum was shipped from Salem to Africa, where it was traded for slaves who were brought to the West Indies to work on sugar plantations.

A Nutmeg Farm

For hundreds of years, many spices were grown on large plantations in Indonesia and other parts of Asia where people were used as slave laborers. By the late 1600s, spices were grown on plantations in the Old and New Worlds. Today, some spices are still grown on large plantations but with paid laborers instead of slaves. Other spices are grown by small-scale, or smallholder, farmers who barely make a living from their work.

Nutmeg and Mace

The spices nutmeg and mace come from an evergreen tree that at one time grew only on a few small islands in Indonesia. Today, the tree is cultivated in Sri Lanka, Sumatra, and Grenada. The nutmeg tree, or *Myristica fragrans,* grows to 40 feet (12 meters) tall on plantations in warm, tropical areas. It takes up to eight years for the tree to bare the mace and nutmeg fruit. The fruit is gathered when it falls to the ground and the mace, or outer husk, is removed, pressed flat and dried on mats. The nutmegs are dried on trays for several weeks until the nutmeg inside rattles against the shell. The shells are then cracked and the nuts are removed.

(above) Nutmeg was traditionally harvested from trees using poles with cages on the end that shake the fruit down.

◀ *Nutmeg fruit looks like apricots on the tree. When the fruit is ready to harvest, the nut inside the fruit bursts, or splits the fruit open.*

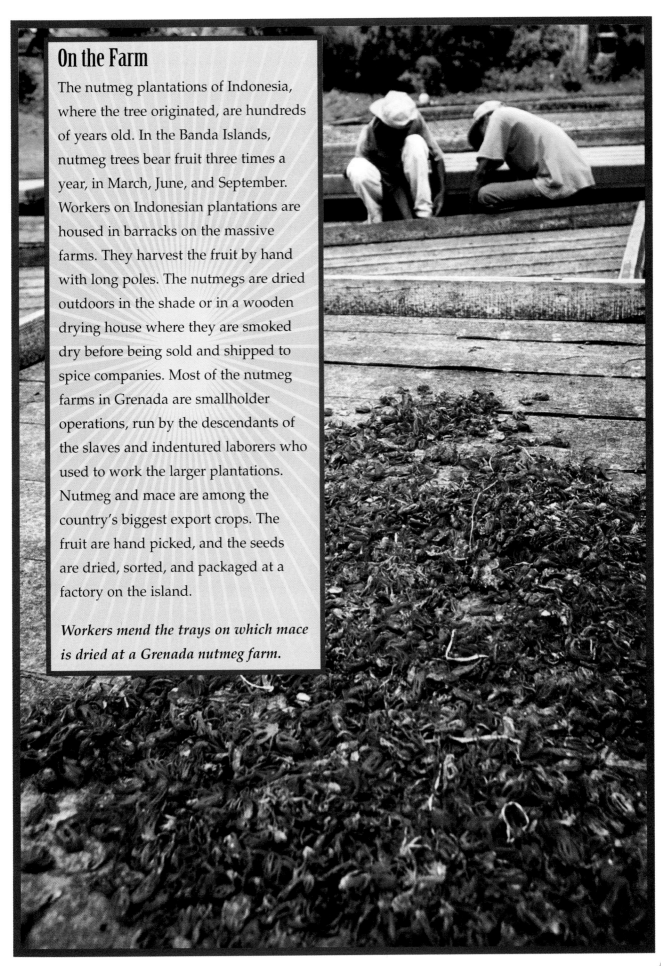

On the Farm

The nutmeg plantations of Indonesia, where the tree originated, are hundreds of years old. In the Banda Islands, nutmeg trees bear fruit three times a year, in March, June, and September. Workers on Indonesian plantations are housed in barracks on the massive farms. They harvest the fruit by hand with long poles. The nutmegs are dried outdoors in the shade or in a wooden drying house where they are smoked dry before being sold and shipped to spice companies. Most of the nutmeg farms in Grenada are smallholder operations, run by the descendants of the slaves and indentured laborers who used to work the larger plantations. Nutmeg and mace are among the country's biggest export crops. The fruit are hand picked, and the seeds are dried, sorted, and packaged at a factory on the island.

Workers mend the trays on which mace is dried at a Grenada nutmeg farm.

Harvesting Other Spices

Black pepper berries are picked about nine months after the pepper vine flowers. Pepper farmers have to know how the spice grows and at which stage to harvest it. Black pepper is picked from the tree while still green. The black berries, or peppercorns, are then allowed to ferment, or ripen off the tree. When ripe, they are dried in the sun until they shrivel and turn color. White peppercorns are the same berries as black peppercorns, but they are allowed to ripen on the vine. The berries are then soaked in water and their outer papery hulls or skins are removed. The grayish peppercorns are then dried until they turn creamy white. Green peppercorns are unripe, or immature berries that are picked and then freeze-dried or packed in brine so that they stay green.

Growing Cloves

Clove trees are slow to bear fruit. They can take up to 20 years to reach maturity, but produce for another 30 years. The trees grow to about 40 to 50 feet (12 to 15 meters) when cultivated. Clove buds are harvested in June and in October, before the flower petals open. The buds are hand-picked by workers who climb the trees and put the cloves into sacks and set them out to dry in the sun where they turn from green to dark brown. On the Moluccan islands of Ternate and Tidor, there are many small home factories where workers remove the stems or twigs from cloves. When dry, the cloves are packaged for shipment to spice companies, or to factories where clove cigarettes are made.

Many different spices, including cloves, cinnamon, pepper, and nutmeg are grown on the island of Zanzibar, in Africa. On this small spice farm, cloves are being dried in the sun.

Cinnamon

Cinnamon trees are grown on small farms, and in the past, on large plantations. At harvest time, cinnamon bark is carefully stripped from the trees, and rolled into sticks. Cinnamon trees take from three to six years from planting to produce bark for harvesting. The bark is then harvested twice a year. In the wild, cinnamon trees grow to great heights, but cultivated cinnamon trees are pruned down two years after planting so the trees will grow branches and twigs that will produce bark. Cassia is another tree that produces spice bark. Workers harvest cassia bark by peeling or lifting it from the tree, often during a rainy season when the tree has been soaked for days. The bark is then dried on mats where it curls as it dries.

Allspice Farms

In Jamaica, where most of the world's allspice is grown, smallholder farmers grow allspice trees along with other tropical crops, including coconuts. Allspice grows wild all over Jamaica. The berries are picked when mature, from August to October. The farmers climb 15 to 20 feet (five to six meters) into the trees to pick the fruit using a pruner. They cut the branches and stems down to help the tree grow thicker the next season. After cutting, farmers remove the berries from the stems by hand and set aside the leaves, which are processed for oil. The berries are dried in the sun for about two weeks. After drying, the berries are sold for export.

(top and right) Cinnamon is harvested from the tree by peeling off the bark. It is then dried.

Spice Trading Today

(above) In some parts of the world, spices are sold fresh in spice markets instead of prepackaged in grocery stores. This spice merchant in Pakistan prepares special spice mixtures for customers.

Thousands of years ago, the spice trade was controlled by merchants from one area of the world. The merchants bought the spices directly from the growers in Asia and brought them to markets in Europe. Later, European countries began to dominate the spice trade by establishing colonies on spice-growing islands, and forcing the islanders to toil in slavery. Today, the spices that make it to our tables are grown on both small-scale farms and on bigger plantations. Most of the spices are sold to major **multinational** spice companies, who package, market, and sell the spices to grocery and other food stores.

Farmers

Farmers who grow spices on a small scale do not make a lot of money for growing and harvesting their crops. When there is too much of one spice on the market, the price drops, but they must still pay for fertilizers to make the soil rich, and pesticides to keep insects away. Spice exporters who can afford to purchase from many spice farmers, and sell to a market thousands of miles away, make more money than farmers. Spice buyers from the major spice companies travel directly where the spices are grown to buy their spices from farmers, or occasionally, spice traders.

Spice-Buying Centers

The United States is the world's top spice buyer, and millions of pounds of spices are imported into the U.S. each year, mostly by spice companies. Imported spices are brought to major ports were they are inspected for cleanliness. Spices must pass the standards of the U.S. Food and Drug Administration and the American Spice Trade Association. The American Spice Trade Association is an organization that promotes the spice industry and spice companies. It formed in 1907, partly in an effort to keep spices pure. Other countries have similar standards for imported spices.

Fair Trade

Within the last ten years, a growing number of spice farmers have been selling their spices to companies and people that guarantee them a fair price for their spices. These companies belong to a group called the Fair Trade Federation. The Federation includes members who buy spices to sell but also agree to follow the rules of fair trade. Those rules include: paying fair wages to workers and farmers, educating buyers of products like spices, helping small farmers to get loans to buy land or improve their businesses, and following farming and processing habits that do not harm the environment.

Some spice farmers in Africa and India have turned to tourism to make more money. They show tourists how spices, such as pepper, are grown in return for a fee.

Glossary

Arabia The southwestern part of the Arabian peninsula, including the present-day countries of Saudi Arabia, Yemen, Oman, Qatar, Bahrain, Kuwait, and United Arab Emirates

aromatic A fragrant herb or plant part

balm An aromatic substance used in healing or made into an ointment or salve

British Empire The lands Britain colonized and ruled over, beginning in the 1600s and lasting until the mid-1900s

Christian A follower of the teachings of Jesus Christ, who Christians believe is God's son

city-state A city, usually of ancient times, that ruled itself

colonies Lands controlled by a distant country

commercial For gain or profit

concessions Business privileges or exclusive rights to sell something

conquer To take over by force

coveted Greatly desired or wanted

dowry The money or property a woman brings to her marriage

empire A group of lands under a single ruler

exotic Something that is from another land

export To sell to another country

extinct No longer in existence

fertile Able to produce abundant crops or vegetation

glands Parts of the body that produce or release substances

Hebrew The people of ancient Israel

herb A non-woody plant

incense A mixture of herbs, plants, and oils that is aromatic when burned

indentured laborers Workers who sign a contract with their employers for a certain amount of time and for passage to another place

intestine A long, tube-shaped part of the body used for digestion

Jesus Christ The man who Christians believe is both God and the son of God

manipulate To influence or control something

multinational Operating in more than one country

native Belonging to a certain place

nobles People with power in a society, usually because of wealth or family titles

plantation A large farm with many workers that usually specializes in growing one main crop

secretion The release of a substance by the body

stigma The tip of the female part of a flower

temperate Climates that do not have extreme weather

thresh To beat a plant to separate the seeds from the straw

transplant To plant seedlings somewhere else

Index

allspice 9, 12, 23, 29

ancient spice trade 4, 6, 7, 8, 9, 10, 12, 13, 14-17

aromatics 13, 16

cinnamon 4, 9, 10, 18, 21, 28, 29

cloves 4, 8, 10, 11, 28

exploration 4, 8, 9, 12, 19, 20-23, 25

ginger 12, 14, 16

mustard 12, 14, 18

New World 6, 9, 12, 21, 22-23, 24, 25

nutmeg 4, 6, 8, 9, 10, 18, 21, 26-27

pepper 4, 7, 9, 10, 12, 17, 18, 25, 28, 31

plantations 6, 9, 21, 22, 23, 24, 25, 26, 27, 29

resins 5, 7, 13, 15

saffron 7, 11, 18

slaves 6, 21, 23, 25

Spice Islands 6, 7, 8, 9, 10, 14, 15, 19, 20, 21, 26, 27

spice harvest 12, 26-27, 28-29

1 2 3 4 5 6 7 8 9 0 Printed in the U.S.A. 4 3 2 1 0 9 8 7 6 5